Animal Crackers

Written by Ken Ross
Illustrated by Pat McCarthy

D1379592

HENDERSON
PUBLISHING PLC

A froggie sat on a lily-pad
Looking up at the sky;
The lily pad broke and the frog fell in,
Water all in his eye.

A rabbit raced a turtle,
You know the turtle won;
And Mister Bunny came in late,
A little hot cross bun.

LUBBLY LIMERICKS

A rhino with a seven foot horn
Was hungry from the day he was born
So he traded his protuberance
For a day of exuberance
In a field filled with fresh fruit and corn.

A chimp with a severe case of fleas
Was so itchy he fell to his knees.
A witchdoctor found him
And with flea-killer drowned him
Until he was clean enough
to return to the trees.

(To be sung to the
tune of
Auld Lang Syne)

On mules we find two legs behind,

And two we find before;

We stand behind before we find

What the two behind be for.

When we're behind the two behind

We find what these be for;

So stand before the two behind,

And behind the two before.

What do you say to a camel when you've made it a cup of tea? One hump or two?

What does it mean when you find a horseshoe? Some poor horse is walking around in his socks.

Which country do kangaroos like best? Roo-mania.

Which animal sticks pins in its coat? A badger.

Three apes went to the barbers. The barber asked the first ape what he wanted. 'A short back and sides,' said the first ape.

The barber then asked the second ape what he wanted. 'I'll have a short back and sides too,' said the second ape.

'And what do you want?' the barber asked the third ape. The third ape smiled, 'Oh, I'll have a long back and big arms please.'

I'm a bear when I take my clothes off
I'm a rabbit without my hair
I'm a horse when I throw my shoes off
I'm a cat when I sit and stare
I'm a gorilla when I beat my chest hard
I'm a fish when I swim in the sea
When I run I'm as fast as a cheetah
When I sting I'm as sharp as a bee
I'm an owl when I act with wisdom
I'm a cow when I grunt and groan
And I'm human when my kingdom
Is a home which all creatures own.

MARY HAD A MENAGERIE

Mary had a little lamb
It had a sooty foot.
And into Mary's bread and jam
Its sooty foot it put.

Mary had a little cow
It fed on safety pins.
And every time she milked the cow
The milk came out in tins.

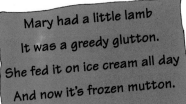

Mary had a little lamb
It was a greedy glutton.
She fed it on ice cream all day
And now it's frozen mutton.

What does a buffalo say when leaving his young boy alone? Bison.

How do fleas travel? They itch-hike.

What do you call a square ox? A box.

What do you call musical insects? Hum-bugs.

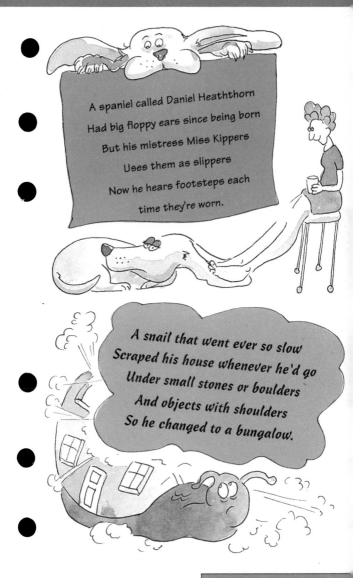

A spaniel called Daniel Heaththorn
Had big floppy ears since being born
But his mistress Miss Kippers
Uses them as slippers
Now he hears footsteps each time they're worn.

A snail that went ever so slow
Scraped his house whenever he'd go
Under small stones or boulders
And objects with shoulders
So he changed to a bungalow.

Best dessert Jelly fish

Hardiest outdoor camper Nightingale

Best in alphabet Bee

Best night-time swimmer Star fish

Tallest in Denmark Great Dane

Best for babies Rattlesnake

Most unfit Puffin

Most expensive animal Deer

Best fighter Slug

Easiest to eat Swallow

Best at number games Dingo

Best on shoes Eel

Speediest animal Swift

Biggest coward Chicken

Best chess player Rook

Best digger Boar

Two snakes went shopping in a supermarket. They thought their bill was wrong and complained.

The bill was checked and found to be correct. 'You know your trouble,' said the supermarket manager - 'you're a lousy pair of adders.'

Ooey gooey was a worm,
A little worm was he,
He sat upon the railway tracks,
The train he did not see.
Ooey gooey!

I went to the animal fair

All the birds and the beasts were there;

The gay baboon by the light of the moon

Was combing his yellow hair.

The monkey fell from his bunk

And dropped on the elephant's trunk.

The elephant sneezed, and went down on his knees

And what became of the monkey, mon-key,

Mon-key, mon-key,

Mon-key, mon-key monk?

A COUPLE OF POMES

A centipede was happy quite,
Until a frog in fun
Said, 'Pray, which leg comes after which?'
This raised her mind to such a pitch,
She lay distracted in a ditch
Considering how to run.

A jolly old bear at the zoo
Could always find something to do.
When it bored him to go
On a walk to and fro,
He reversed it, and walked fro and to.

What do you give
a sick bird?

Tweetment.

What do you give
a sick pig?

Oinkment.

What do you give a
sick frog?

A hoperation.

Where do you
take a sick bee?   To waspital.

Where do you take
a sick labrador?

To the dogtor.

Where do you take a sick horse?

To horsepital.

Where do rabbits get their glasses?

At the hoptician.

How do you get a pig to hospital?

In a hambulance.

Why was the chicken sick?

It had people pox.

What do you give a horse with a cold?

Cough stirrup.

WOMAN: There're about forty cows in our garden, George! George, there's about forty cows in our garden!
GEORGE: I herd.

Where do cow astronauts go? To the moooon.

Why did the cow lie on its back? To trip low flying ducks.

What's black and white and goes "eh?" A monolingual cow trying to speak to the one that speaks five languages.

I'm a knock-kneed chicken,
I'm a bow-legged sparrow,
Missed my bus bus so I went by barrow.
I went to the cafe for my
dinner and my tea,
Too many radishes - hic! pardon me.

Heard about the bird that
scored at soccer then sunk
a very long putt at golf?
It was a goalden eagle.

How do cockerels
tell off their children?
Cock-a-doodle-don't.

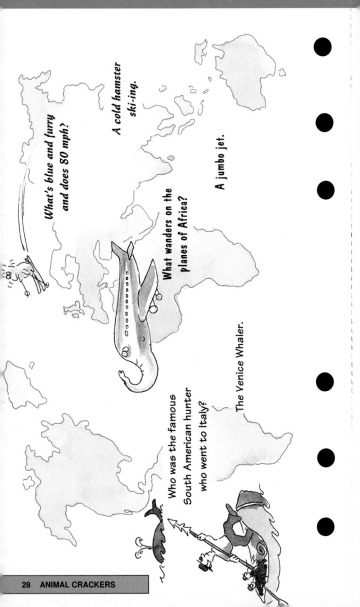

What's blue and furry and does 80 mph?

A cold hamster ski-ing.

What wanders on the planes of Africa?

A jumbo jet.

Who was the famous South American hunter who went to Italy?

The Venice Whaler.

An ostrich who buried his head
Was alarmed when his mouth wasn't fed
So he dug in the place
Where he'd buried his face
Only to find the head of a camel instead.

A mole who annoyed old farmer Rose
By making hills where his barley crop grows
Was hit with a huge log
Then sniffed by the sheepdog
And now he's a mole on its nose.

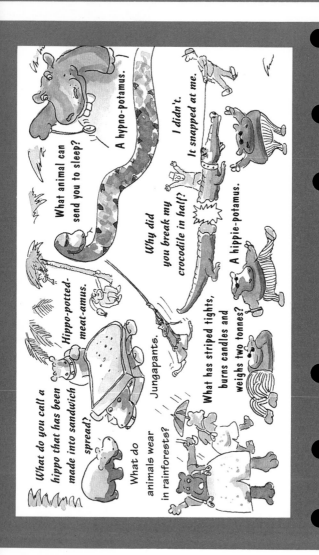

A VERY LONG JOKE

An elephant goes to Mars. When he gets there he finds that accommodation is very expensive, so decides to get a job. At the job centre there is a long queue of Martians. The elephant waits until he can see what jobs are on offer.

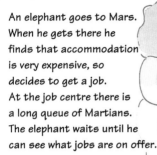

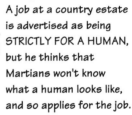

A job at a country estate is advertised as being STRICTLY FOR A HUMAN, but he thinks that Martians won't know what a human looks like, and so applies for the job.

At his interview the Martian says he needs proof that he is human. 'No problem,' says the elephant. 'I can show you my trunk - all humans have trunks. They wear them, and they keep possessions inside them. I come from Tuscany in France - that is in Europe.'

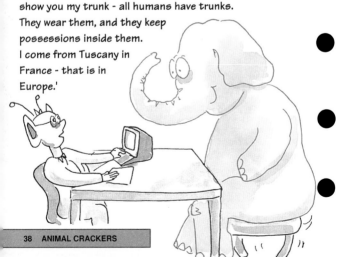

The Martian looked at him. 'But I thought humans were pink?' 'We are pink when young, but when we grow old we go grey.'

'Fine,' said the Martian, 'then the job is yours.' The visitor smiled and asked exactly what the job entailed.

'Oh, it's easy,' laughed the Martian, 'it's a simple job, cleaning out the elephant compound.'

A BABOON'S BEDTIME BOOKS

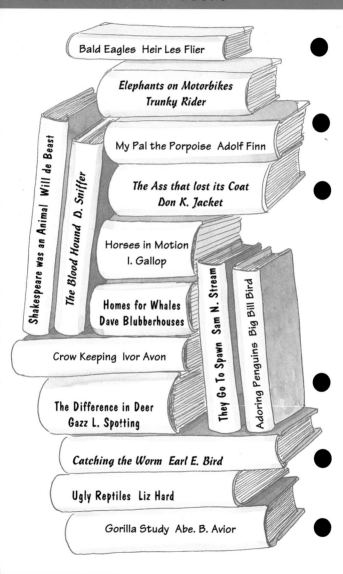

Bald Eagles Heir Les Flier

Elephants on Motorbikes
Trunky Rider

My Pal the Porpoise Adolf Finn

The Ass that lost its Coat
Don K. Jacket

Horses in Motion
I. Gallop

Homes for Whales
Dave Blubberhouses

Crow Keeping Ivor Avon

The Difference in Deer
Gazz L. Spotting

Catching the Worm Earl E. Bird

Ugly Reptiles Liz Hard

Gorilla Study Abe. B. Avior

Shakespeare was an Animal Will de Beast

The Blood Hound D. Sniffer

They Go To Spawn Sam N. Stream

Adoring Penguins Big Bill Bird

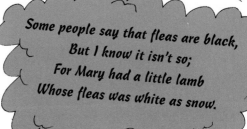

Some people say that fleas are black,
But I know it isn't so;
For Mary had a little lamb
Whose fleas was white as snow.

East is East and West is West,
Though this may not seem relevant.
We all know how to milk a cow,
But you can't muck about with an elephant.

THE RHINO POME

No one for spelling at a loss is
Who boldly spells Rhinocerosses;
I've known a few (I can't say lots)
Who call the beast Rhinocerots,
Though they are not so bad, say I,
As those who say Rhinoceri.
One I have heard (O holy Moses!)
Who plainly said Rhinoceroses,
Another one - a brilliant boy -
Insists that it's Rhinoceroi -
The moral that I draw from these is
The plural's what one darn well pleases.

REAL DEFINITIONS

KINGFISHER monarch who likes angling.

WALRUS the perimeter of Mr Ross's house.

MARSUPIAL eel that swims in ma's soup.

CHIPMUNK a monk who has turned into a chip

ANACONDA Anna Bloggs before she married Mr Conda.

KANGAROO cry of a Scottish prisoner.

DOLPHIN a skinny doll

SWAN abbreviation for 'it is one'

WEASEL ghastly noise from chest

MAGPIE a pie made from magazines

POLECAT a pussy who stands for parliament

VOTE POLECAT

ANOTHER LONG ONE

A woman bought a sheep dog from a pet shop. She took it home, and a few days later the sheep dog was dead.

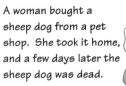

The woman went back to the pet shop and this time asked for a sausage dog. A few days later that too was dead.

When the woman returned again to the pet shop, the owner was curious.

What do you want another dog for?' he said.
'The first two are dead,' said the woman.
'What happened to the sheep dog then?' he asked.
'My husband made him into a woolly jumper.' The pet shop owner was amazed.

'And I suppose your husband ate the sausage dog,' he said. 'Yes,' said the woman. 'So what do you want this time?' 'A bull dog,' said the woman.

'Well, if your husband can't tell the difference between a sheep dog and a sheep, he surely won't be able to tell the difference between a bull dog and a bull.'

PETS

'It's worse than that,' she said, 'he's going to milk it and call it Daisy.'

A crocodile went in an off-licence and asked for a can of beer.

'I'm not serving you,' said the assistant. 'Why?' asked the crocodile.

'Because,' the man said, 'you're under eighteen.'

What do gorillas do with old banana skins?

Throw them away, I expect.